REFLECTIVE HUMAN SOCIALIZATION & GOVERNANCE IN THE 21ST CENTURY FOR INDIGENOUS & ABORIGINAL PEOPLES

ABSTRACT

Many indigenous peoples today are attempting to communicate their presence to the independent governments that control their ancestral lands, or lands that they legally occupy; and to other governments around the world. These international type communications can reach legal standing if you have legal standing by and from an "Acknowledged" and or "Recognized" agency with standing and then only if one knows how to use them. Most importantly, you must be able to produce legitimate international, factual support backed by an internationally Acknowledged or Recognized Indigenous entity (or Government). We shall explore these concepts in these lessons. These lessons are for the education of our clan, our family, and the Clan Mothers, Chiefs, officials, educators, students, and all nationals of the Mund Bareefan Clan - INAAN. Indigenous peoples around the world have always used what we described as "Reflective Human Socialization" also called "Reflective Humanism", as the means to set our moral and ethical standards and to develop and govern our environments.

*Note This is not a solicitation, we are not seeking new nationals to our Clan. In the United States and internationally we "are" Mund Bareefan Clan, an acknowledged indigenous family, also called MT. 'Arafat Clan. We are Guale-Yamassee, we are the Executive Tribe of an association of Clans, Bands, and Tribes. Our association is called "The Indigenous Native American Association of Nations".

US Copyright ©TM 2019 by S.G. Chief Black Hawk Thunderbird
ROYAL THUNDERBIRD INTERPRIZES
in association with
Saqur publishing
INARS catalog number: 11062001
ISBN # 978-0-9857375-6-6

Table of Contents

Introduction..5
Lesson One-Reflective Humanism...............................7
Enter-Governmental Communications........................8
Internationally Recognized Legal
Status..9
Recitation of Life- The Southern
Cult..15
Frequency Earth- Mother in Crisis.............................16
Mund Bareefan and the Yamassee Union of
1995..19
Mund Bareefan Clan..21
Action in its Legal Context..22
International Documents (Instruments).....................23
THE HAGUE CONFERENCE. PRIVATE INTERNATIONAL
LAW...24
Convention 107..31

Istagwaad
Introduction

We write for the education of our family and the Indigenous Native American Association of Nations peoples. Within these lessons, we will learn much about the hidden information of the dark-skinned indigenous people of Ancient America, and our re-emergence on the international scene. We will unlock the past for you in a way not done for you by ones of our own.

If you are looking for religious, spiritual, or mystical incite/vision, then don't look for it in the information that we are about to impart upon you; the religious, spiritual, and mystical incites has already been given to us, and we acknowledge them from before.

We will tell you-all of who we are as a people in America and in the international world.

On a program on PBS television about African American ancestry in February 2008, the host of this program implied that there were no indigenous "black" people here in America. I don't think that he meant to, but he did.

In this lesson we will make that matter clear.

You all will learn about our Proto-Native American ancestors, a proud and gallant people of the Southern Cult Tribes of southeast North America, our homeland.

These lessons make clear that all the Indigenous Clans like the Guale, Yamassee, Creek, Cherokee, Seminole, and others of Southeastern America from Virginia, to all the Carolinas down to Florida, and from the Atlantic Ocean to the Mississippi River; the Olmec civilizations of Mexico; to the indigenous societies of South and Central America were and are one people with different clans and tribes before the European Settlers came.

We, the Mund Bareefan Clan and many other of our brethren have cohabited among the African American community and are part of the African American experience, however, the history of Black Native Americans and Africans, predates the Trans-Atlantic Slave Trade, and includes an African and American History that the European settlers and their successors omit.

When a lesson/study of the presence of blacks in America begins with African slavery in the 1500s thru the 1800s, then back to the Trans-Atlantic Slave Trade, our true indigenous ancestry gets misplaced somewhere. It is incomplete.

In these lessons, we the descendants of the "Southern-Cult" will learn of how and when our ancestors arrived here in America.

However, when we research His-Story of France, England, and Spain in America from about 1107 AD through the 1700s, we find that these French, European and Spanish, and other visitors were greeted by the "Southern-Cult", as the newcomers arrived at the Americas.

We hope that you all learn from and enjoy the lesson.

Thank you-all, SGC

These lessons are for the education of my family, the Clan Mothers, Chiefs, officials, educators, students and all nationals of the Mund Bareefan Clan/INAAN

Lesson I:

Reflective Humanism: Unlike with the anthropocentric paradigm central to most governments and religions of today, Reflective Humanism, lived by indigenous people for centuries is directed by "human intellect", from the collective, not from the top down or from some individual sovereign entity.

You might say, that is the way the United States and many other governments operate. Well, somewhat. The difference is that <u>many governments</u> today operate according to as they say, "what God wills", or "what Allah wills", or "Jehovah wills" for their morals and their ethical standards instead of human intellect. This works well for the religious/spiritual paradigms, but not so well with government. Yet in courts, civil, and criminal proceedings, one is expected to swear an oath on a holy book.

In our courts, as in our government offices, the oath or swear in- the affirmation, is to our "INAAN Constitution", the highest non-religious laws of the land. Courts are not Holy. Holy books should not be used for secular courts or government practices.

Let's make this simple. The tribal courts and/or tribal councils meet, consider and make rules based in our Constitution. The universe, time, and experience has granted man intellectual capacity to make tools like constitutions to aid in the building of harmonious, safe, well-balanced environments for the people, and with the surrounding nature. This ethic is our small part in helping maintain the balance in the trio: Earth-Atmosphere-Universe. As above. So below.

Some have construed our efforts as part of the sovereignty movement. It is not. When you fight the current sovereignty battles, we hear about today in and against the US, you fight a battle that can only be won by the officials that are charged by the specific government that made its codex's, manuals, rules and regulations; its practices and procedures for its own internal security against its adversaries; and they set the protocols for <u>its internal implementation, and that's the way it works</u>. We should be so attentive with our internal and local affairs.

Many indigenous people today are attempting to communicate their presence to the independent governments that control their ancestral lands or lands that they legally occupy, and to other governments around the world.

Inter-Governmental communications These international type communications can reach legal standing <u>if you have established legal standing</u> by way of self-determination, and with and from an "Acknowledged" and or recognized Indigenous agency with standing, and then only if one knows how to use them. Still be prepared to fight for your rights, but this time with the best tools. We have begun to achieve this capacity for our Clan, and are working to improve.

<u>*Note: In the United States and internationally we are Mund Bareefan Clan. We are Guale-Yamassee Indigenous Native Americans, with the legal acknowledgment of the legal capacity of self-determination and self-governance. We are "IN FACT" an Acknowledged Indigenous tribe/family, acknowledged both Federally and by the sevel States in the United States of America.</u>

<u>We are also called MT. 'Arafat Clan in English. Our association is called "The Mund Bareefan Clan Indigenous Native American Association of Nations".</u>

To others who may be reading this lesson, know that if your clan (family) or group of indigenous people seek to communicate your issues to other governments, or in a court of law, you should use an International approach.

As an indigenous people in the United States, we must do this together. If you are an INAAN national, do not be tricked by those who cannot produce legitimately approved certification "of their own", from an "Acknowledged" and or Recognized Indigenous Government Agency, with US Federal and or State "Acknowledgement" of such status; or US "Federal Recognition". There are several "Acknowledged" and or Recognized Indigenous Governmental Agencies.

Internationally recognized legal national status

Q. Can you tell me your internationally recognized legal national status in the United States and around the world?

A. We are indigenous. Most people in the United States, melanin dominant or not, are legally documented US citizens. That's not a bad thing, it's simply the reality. As such, you don't have an internationally recognized nationality as members of an autonomous, indigenous, self-determined people.

Many people are unaware of the laws of nationality. When we are children, we take on the nationality our parents have chosen. What we ignore, or are not taught, is that when we are grown, we have the right, the obligation, to declare who we are. If you don't, you continue to carry the nationality designation assigned at birth.

"Indigenous people" in the United States have had our nationality and ethnicity chosen and assigned by colonizing governments for hundreds of years. This reality has almost caused some of us to lose our original birthright, original ethnicity to this land, and nationality as Indigenous Native Americans.

We use ethnic titles like Colored, Negro, Black American, Chicano, Latino American, Moorish American, Nuwaubian, White American, African American, (or any derivative thereof,) Muslim, Christian, and there are others. These are good honorable things to be. Some of these titles we consider national/international designations as autonomous, but they are not. None of the above titles gives international recognition as Autonomous Peoples in the United States. Well... maybe white? The following is Gualean Law, and international law:

1. Indigenous Native American Association of Nations Constitution "Bill of Rights"
   Article 5:

> <u>Everyone has the right to a nationality. No one shall be arbitrarily deprived of his nationality nor denied the right to change his nationality. Every indigenous individual has the right to a nationality.</u>

2. UN Declaration of the Rights of Indigenous People Article 6:

> Every indigenous individual has the right to a nationality.

3. UN UNIVERSAL DECLARATION OF HUMAN RIGHTS

   Article 15:

   > (a) Everyone has the right to a nationality.
   > (b) No one shall be arbitrarily deprived of his nationality nor denied the right to change his nationality.

4. Indigenous and Tribal Peoples' Rights in Practice: A guide to ILO Convention No. 169 Article 6:
   > Every indigenous individual has the right to a nationality.

Simply put, as indigenous and aboriginal peoples, we have the right and the obligation to choose.

Maybe you're Indigenous, or maybe you're African, or maybe you are African American, or you may be a combination of all of the above. Considering the right to self-determination,

it's your right to choose. There is historically documented evidence that Africans were the first to come to this land. They are called the Anu/Twa people of West Africa. How long ago? The records show 51,700 years or more ago they landed at one location in North America now called Mexico and three locations in South America.

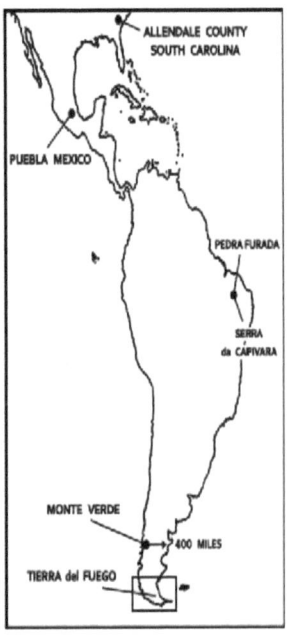

Seven hundred years later another expedition would leave again from West Africa and landed at the place now called South Carolina. Their descendants have spread around the southeast. They developed tribes and clans, some speaking the Hitichi language. There is some question as to the specific language of the Guale/Yamassee. Now, our chosen languages are Gualean Yamassic, English, and Spanish. Gualean Yamassic has some Semitic sounds as in Hitichi. For more about our language, see our Gualean Yamassic grammar books. We are all of the people of "El Janub Nasfa Kara A'dut" or "The Southern Cult".

After thousands of years of occupation of this land, we and our brethren across this land reserve "the first rights" of "the first people". We are Indigenous to the land called the United States of America.

We know that we have Ancient African blood, and we declare that we are not African. Historically and legally our family/clan is Indigenous to America. One of the oldest names for our land is Guale. Guale, an ancient name for Coastal Georgia and the sounding islands before foreign

Europeans settlers arrived at her shores. Altamaha, Capital of the Yamassee, is on Guale land near today's Darian, Georgia. The most Principle Chief of the Guale carried the name "Chief Guale". His Chiefdom (capitol) was on the Island. The most Principle Chief of the Yamassee was named "Altamaha", same as the nearest river. So, ancient people from Africa occupied both North and South America for thousands of years before the Europeans came to what were to them new lands. Many of the Europeans first thought the land was "India"? Well, at least that's what was taught.

Like many other melanin dominant humans in the Americas, our ancient ancestors the Twa-Anu people from West Africa came to this land thousands of years ago on boats. Most of our family (Mund Bareefan Clan) remain on the land in South Carolina, Georgia, and Alabama. Many from our families migrated north during the industrial revolution. Some remain in the north, some have returned home to the Southeast.

Descendants of the Twa-Anu people from West Africa, set up their first major settlements in what is now South Carolina. They then spread through the southeast in America and became known as the "Southern Cult".

The action taken by our ancestors caused them to be the first to occupy areas that became known as Coastal Georgia, inclusive of the surrounding Islands and what is now North and South Carolina, and over to the Mississippi River. Historically they are also called Mound Builders, and Mississippians.

Mund Bareefan Clan's direct family ancestors lived and are buried on the land. Many family members still occupy these areas continuously from those days, until this very day; in Alabama, Allendale County South Carolina, Barnwell County South Carolina, Darlington County South Carolina, and in Yemassee South Carolina. These facts and our declaration is the basis of our lawful nationality as an Indigenous Native American Clan.

Humans on this continent and all around the world had developed societies, clans, tribes, and alliances. Our ancestors lived in systems that were based in abilities granted to humans by "Father Sky" and "Mother Earth" to aid the humans with the development of well balanced, harmonious societies, which are based in human intellect called "Reflective Humanism".

Internationally, we are the Indigenous Native American Association of Nations. Today, Indigenous Native American Association of Nations peoples are Black, White, Christian, Muslim, Hebrew, Nuwaubian, Moors, and others; some may be Atheist. You may be a Mason or an Eastern-Star, you may belong to any social, civic, or religious institution you wish. None of these things matters to your legal nationality. Do you get it? We'll talk more about that in other lessons.

Recitation Life "The Sothern Cult".
Istartaal Hayuh "El Janub Nasfa Kara".

We are pure energy; a single thought manifesting with a double movement in the cosmos.

We are kin to the ethers, the fire, the air, wind, the water, and the earth.

We are conceived within the cycles of time within this Universe. With the turn of time, we manifest, brought through by the nature of and for this planet.

Our essence has grown from the water and soil of 'Ammatum' Earth our Mother.

Our essence is shared among many, stemming from the branches of a great tree that sprang forth from this land.

Our branches extend, and our foliage continues to spread like a canopy across this Land now called America. We Exist. We are called 'The Southern Cult'.   We are "Indigenous" ... SGC

Reflective Humanism by Dr. Raymundo Lopez Ortiz Grand Chief and Consul General to Mexico for INAAN: "In the history of indigenous peoples our sages describe that human behavior and thought patterns were in universal cosmic perspectives;" our perspectives surpass the underlying (current) anthropocentrism ... "With anthropocentrism, most of the current ideologies are centered in humanity's liberation yet they act as if they are unaware of the need for liberation of the cosmos". In other words, the Universe and the planet, simply put "Nature" has granted "intellect" and "common sense" to humans, which gives us the capacity to develop environments with rules, regulations, codes of conduct etc. that will be beneficial to all in the environment.

What is anthropocentrism? "It is human perceptions of morality, based in foreign, supernatural or extraterrestrial influence or authority. This is in most religions and governments of today.

"Most of the current ideologies are centered in humanity's liberation yet they act as if they are unaware of the need for liberation of the cosmos..."

"At the same time our socialization; our social "Reflective Humanism" (which is human based perceptions of morality), enables us to liberate and to recognize beyond the ideologies prevalent in many current doctrines globally, and can free us from their financial feudalism..."

Concepts of Reflective Humanism, Humanitarianism, Anthropocentrism, even those of Atheism and others should cooperate in the construction of the new society.

The MBC are the descendants of a once thought to be vanquished Guale/Yamassee people. We have stepped up and out of the midst of American History, African-American History, and American

Indian History, once again to claim indigenous rights as one expression of self-determination, law, and self-governance.

The conquering European settler nations declared us Guale and Yamassee extinct because they wanted (want) our lands. Despite this, we remain, and we declare that the alleged extinction has not been the extinction of our biogenetic identity, nor the existence of our flesh, blood, soul, and spirit; nor of our Indigenous Native American character and ancestry.

Rather it was a failed attempt by the European Settlers to cause the loss of consciousness of our Indigenous Native American origins and national identity.

We INAAN people are descendants of a pre-Columbian Indigenous society, captured into slavery on our own lands here in what is now America.

To survive as a people and to one day rebuild our nation, black Proto Guale-Yamassee mixed and married into other black clans and tribes like Mexicans, the Dravidians of India, Seminoles, the Creeks, the Cherokees, the Washitaw, as well as our brethren the black African Slaves.

Online writer Paul Barton offers the following:

"Among the other Black nations who existed in the Americas before Columbus and long before Christ were the Jamassee (Yamassee), who had a large kingdom in the southeastern United States. Their descendants were among the first Blacks of pre-Columbian American origins who fell victim to kidnapping for the purpose of enslavement. Blacks of South America, the Caribbean, and Central America were also attacked and enslaved based on a Pontifax passed during the mid-1400's by the Church hierarchy giving the Europeans the go-

> *ahead to enslave all "Children of Ham" found in the newly discovered territories.* <u>*The descendants of the Jamassee are the millions of Blacks who live in Alabama, Georgia, South Carolina, and northern Florida.*</u>*"*

Our ancestors left Africa centuries ago. They migrated to America and have occupied this land permanently and continuously for thousands of years. Now, neither Africa nor Europe are North America. In this day in time, their respective peoples (black or white) are not the original people of this land.

If you have been studying, you know that Africans and indigenous Americans have been visiting, doing commerce and marrying for thousands of years. Then one day the Europeans bought and or captured and brought the black Africans to America to make slaves in America. They forced and mingled <u>black Africans</u> with the <u>black Native Americans</u> in America to dilute our stock or make dark-skinned indigenous people of this continent extinct. What <u>a thought</u>.

The forced mingling was taking place in North America on indigenous land upon indigenous people. In accord with laws of man and nature, with the forced mingling taking place upon Native Americans in American, the Africans, who by the way were sold into slavery and were now residing with indigenous slaves; the Africans become Native American, not the other way around. Even more, we are of the very similar phenotypic origins. How could you tell the differences? You couldn't. Over time, the European settlers made laws trying to replace the indigenous people or to make us a forgotten people.

This was a bad <u>thought</u>; this was a <u>thought</u> of <u>ethnic cleansing</u>. It was a <u>thought</u> that gave birth to a crime against nature. We know that thoughts have weight. <u>This thought</u> would cause hundreds of thousands of indigenous people to carry a burden that has weighed us down for hundreds of years.

As the result of the genocidal motives flowing from that thought, we MBC/INAAN people, descendants of the people of the Southern Cult, find ourselves on a quest, a mission to answer the call of our ancestors and their energies to rebuild our societies in peace and harmony. That is the mission that rages through our flesh and blood and in our bones.

Mund Bareefan and the Yamassee union of 1995:

Chief Black Thunderbird Eagle, Principal Chief of the Yamassee Union in 1995 acknowledged Mt. Arafat amongst the Yamassee Union upon the original charter of our clan in that year. We relocated from Philadelphia, Pennsylvania in the Northeast, to Eatonton, Georgia in the southeast in the Spring of 1997. Our families are originally from the Southeast. We tried to return a few years before but couldn't make it happen. With these new developments, we felt that we were more than ready to make a successful return, so we did.

In October 1997 a delegation from "The Black Light", who were from the Security Dept. of the Yamassee Native Americans (check the original constitution of 1992 cover page), visited our home in Eatonton, Georgia and politely asked us to leave town when they learned Mt. Arafat was studying and mastering the Yamassee Constitution of 1992. They weren't so polite with others.

Mund Bareefan was informed by Security, that the Native American issues were no longer to be part of their immediate agenda. Soon thereafter, Mund Bareefan Clan was informed by the Black Light that their Native American issues would fall under the Yamassee Native American Moors of the Creek Nation, and that they were applying for recognition with the BIA. Don't believe me check it out.

The Yamassee Native American Moors of The Creek Nation has since gone to sleep even though Chief Black Thunderbird Eagle, their Grand Chief, has given his blessing, recognition, and acknowledgment that Mund Bareefan Clan is the official indigenous authority for his people.

Our recognition by Chief Black Eagle would cause friction. So, it was upon agreement between the two Chiefs, as is Native American custom, our Clan-Mund Bareefan Clan, became sister clans; but Mund Bareefan would have to carry its own burden towards self-determination; self-governing.

On March 2nd, 2003, the elders and people of Mund Bareefan Clan declared Grand Chief Black-Hawk Thunderbird, Supreme Grand Chief of our "MBC/INAAN" Clan.

<u>MBC/INAAN is neither a club nor fraternity. MBC/INAAN is not an order, nor a church. As individuals, we may belong to any of the above type organizations as this a matter of personal self-determination, which all man has a right to.</u>

Some of our Clan members are of "The 'Gualean Order of The Masters (formerly the Guale-Yamassee Church of Christ). Others of our chiefs, clan mothers and nationals are Moors, Christian, Muslim, Yoruba, and Buddhists. Some may be Atheist or agnostic; that's personal business unrelated to their legal nationality. MBC/INAAN is the custodian of <u>a non-religious government</u> for Guale/Yamassee Native Americans and the Indigenous Native American Association of Nations.

Mund Bareefan Clan:

Mund Bareefan Clan acts to secure the venue, jurisdiction, and competent lawful United States acknowledgment to implement our right to self-determination.

Mund Bareefan Clan undertook a <u>legal action</u> whereby the official Government for our clan presented Tribal Documents in the form of a "constructive proposal" exclusively drafted by House Thunderbird. The proposal (also referred to as the Blue-back) was first filed and acknowledged in the State of Georgia, March 3rd, 2003.

On February 11th, 2004, the proposal was annexed by The US Department of State; bearing the official endorsement of the US Secretary of State, which notifies all United States government jurisdictions and the international community of the presence of the (MBC/INAAN) Indigenous Native American Government

On October 12, 2004, we also received written confirmation from US Department of State Authentication office, regarding a dispute between one of our nationals and an employer. Our National was using our authenticated identification for legal identification to seek employment.

The quote below is part of an e-correspondence between a Mund Bareefan National "Sean Henry-Bey", a Georgia employer, and the US Department of State Authentication Office. Sean Henry-Bey was a INAAN Chief during his tenure with our "At-Sik Hata" Village, in Macon Georgia.

US Department of State, Authentication office stating in part ...

"the statement on our certificates "full faith and credit" is in acknowledgment of the States certificate to the document; and has sufficient legal value through State and Federal sevels for use in other countries and in this country."

Action in its legal Context: Let's define the action MBC undertook. Action as defined in Black's Law Dictionary 7th Edition: Action. "1. <u>The process of doing something; conduct or behavior.</u> 2. <u>A thing done; Act (1)</u> 3. A civil or criminal judicial proceeding. "An action has been defined to be an ordinary proceeding in a court of justice by which one party prosecutes another party for enforcement or protection of a right, the redress or prevention of a wrong, Or the punishment of a public offense."

The Mund Bareefan proposal is the legal document whereby M.B.C. took Action, def 1, 2 &3 to secure indigenous rights for MBC/INAAN peoples, and lands in accord with statutes, articles and other provisions set forth by our MBC/INAAN Constitution.

Also, with the above defined document(s) The Indigenous Native American Association of Nations is developing operational and administrative procedures for setting a reconstituted MBC/INAAN Government; to bring together again long-lost clans and families; and to bring national identities for the increasing establishment of new institutions and the re-animation of our Native American consciousness, culture and identity.

Despite the attempts of European settlers to destroy our culture and identity through slavery and racism, The Guale-Yamassee have endured to continue the Guale-Yamassee struggles of old, in modern day times, through legal action. We are old school. We live "as kin". In other words, we live of, for, and by each other. Remember that? Are you there? Are we ready for that?

International Documents (Instruments)

Consider the Universal Declaration of Human Rights

The Universal Declaration of Human Rights was framed in 1945, and ratified in 1948, under great influence from Eleanor Roosevelt, Chair of the United Nations Human Rights Commission and wife of US President Franklin D. Roosevelt.

World War II was devastating around the world. No one wanted to see so much destruction among the people and their respective lands. The people suffered many human tragedies. Eleanor Roosevelt would lead the brigade to achieve International consensus for the committee's cause.

The United Nations Commission decided to do something that had not been done since Cyrus the Great. They made a codex and named it The Universal Declaration of Human Rights set in anthropocentric principles. It would guide their actions and communications.

A commission was formed at the United Nations. Much of Eleanor Roosevelt's and the UN's Commission for Human Rights campaign would become human rights law for many peoples around the world. Indigenous peoples, however, were left under the jurisdiction of colonizing governments. Well, don't forget the European colonizers got concepts of human rights from people of color. Think about that. Things that makes you go, hmmm.

The next few years were dedicated to perfecting the operation. By 15 July 1951, STATUTE 01: OF THE HAGUE CONFERENCE ON PRIVATE INTERNATIONAL LAW Entered into force.

THE HAGUE CONFERENCE ON PRIVATE INTERNATIONAL LAW...(Entered into force on 15 July 1955)

"The Governments of the countries hereinafter specified: the Federal Republic of Germany, Austria, Belgium, Denmark, Spain, Finland, France, Italy, Japan, Luxembourg, Norway, the Netherlands, Portugal, the United Kingdom of Great Britain and Northern Ireland, Sweden and Switzerland;

In view of the permanent character of the Hague Conference on Private International Law; Desiring to stress that character; Having, to that end, deemed it desirable to provide the Conference with a Statute; Have agreed 58 upon the following provisions:

Article 1 The purpose of the Hague Conference is to work for the progressive unification of the rules of private international law.

Article 2

(1) Members of the Hague Conference on Private International Law are the States which have already

participated in one or more Sessions of the Conference and which accept the present Statute.

(2)   Any other State, the participation of which is from a judicial point of view of importance for the work of the Conference, may become a Member. The admission of new Member States shall be decided upon by the Governments of the participating States, upon the proposal of one or more of them, by a majority of the votes cast, within a period of six months from the date on which that proposal is submitted to the Governments".

As of 30 June 2005, in addition to the founding Member States mentioned in the Preamble, the following States had accepted the Statute: Albania, Argentina, Australia, Belarus, Bosnia and Egypt, Estonia, Georgia, Greece, Hungary, Iceland, Ireland, Israel, Jordan, Republic of Korea, Latvia, Lithuania, Malaysia, Malta, Mexico, Monaco, Morocco, New Zealand, Panama, Paraguay, Peru, Poland, Romania, Russian Federation, Serbia and Montenegro, Slovak Republic, Slovenia, South Africa, Sri Lanka, Suriname, The former Yugoslav Republic of Macedonia, Turkey, Ukraine, United States of America, Uruguay, Venezuela.

Having acquired the above knowledge lead MBC to a question; How do we get in this club?

Where Did the Conventional Applications of Universal Human Rights Begin?

"In small places, close to home—so close and so small that they cannot be seen on any maps of the world. Yet they are the world of the individual person; the neighborhood he lives in; the school or college he attends; the factory, farm or office where he works. Such are the places where every man, woman, and child seek equal justice, equal opportunity, equal dignity without discrimination. Unless these rights have meaning there, they have little meaning anywhere. Without concerted citizen action to uphold them close to home, we shall look in vain for progress in the larger world." written by Eleanor Roosevelt, wife of US President Franklin D. Roosevelt, and Chair of the United Nations Commission, that wrote the Universal Declaration of Human Rights in 1948. They took a page from Cyrus the Great.

"The Cyrus Cylinder (539 B.C.) Cyrus the Great, the first king of Persia. In 539 B.C., the armies of Cyrus the Great, conquered the city of Babylon. It was his next actions that marked a major advance for Man. He freed the slaves, declared that all people had the right to choose their own religion, and established racial equality. These and other decrees were recorded on a baked-clay cylinder in the Akkadian language with cuneiform script... this ancient record has now been recognized as the world's first charter of human rights. It is translated into all six official languages of the United Nations and its provisions parallel the first four Articles of the Universal Declaration of Human Rights ...

The Spread of Human Rights in the Western society came from Africa and then Asia...

The idea of human rights spread from Babylon quickly to India, Greece and eventually Rome. There the concept of 'natural law' arose, in observation of the fact that people tended to follow certain unwritten laws in the course of life, and Roman law was based on rational ideas derived from the nature of things...

Documents asserting individual rights, such as the Magna Carta (1215), the Petition of Right (1628), the US Constitution (1787), the French Declaration of the Rights of Man and of the Citizen (1789), and the US Bill of Rights (1791)".

Okay, Cyrus the Great, was a Persian King born between 590 and 580 BC. Some western historians say Cyrus II, is accredited for the first declaration of human rights thousands of years ago. This is excepted fact.

For those of you who don't know, Persia was the name for the Indigenous Nation that we call Iran today which at that time included Egypt. but... Let's see what was going on in some other places on the planet at that time.

559 "BC" that would be around 2,576 years ago. Well, in or around 2,576 years ago and prior to that, there were humans living on every continent on the planet. Many of the people were indigenous to most if not all the places (land masses) upon which they live or had occupied for thousands of years prior. Places like Africa, Australia, India, and Sri Lanka. How about "America"? Look at the map of below of towns and Chiefdoms, Tribes, and villages in America for hundreds, and some even thousands of years before the Europeans came. Remember all these peoples practiced socialization.

26

The map below was acquired from:

INDIGENOUS PEOPLES RESOURCES distribute educational resources that celebrate the lives, culture, and history of Indigenous peoples around the world, including Native American, First Nations, Inuit, and Aboriginal Australians

Our Governments, (Clans, our Tribes, alliances, and associations), were not considered as parties to their new Declaration. Those governments only see us as under their jurisdictions. Colonizing governments saw their captives as less in intelligence, not capable of comprehending complex governing. Even worse in America, we became seen as less than human.

Preamble UNITED NATIONS Universal Declaration of Human Rights

Whereas it is essential to promote the development of friendly relations between nations,

Whereas the peoples of the United Nations have in the Charter reaffirmed their faith in fundamental human rights, in the dignity and worth of the human person and in the equal rights of men and women and have determined to promote social progress and better standards of life in larger freedom,

Whereas Member States have pledged themselves to achieve, in cooperation with the United Nations, the promotion of universal respect for and observance of human rights and fundamental freedoms,

Whereas a common understanding of these rights and freedoms is of the greatest importance for the full realization of this pledge,

UNITED NATIONS | Universal Declaration of Human Rights

"Now, therefore, The General Assembly proclaims this Universal Declaration of Human Rights as a common standard of achievement for all peoples and all nations, to the end that every individual and every organ of society, keeping this Declaration constantly in mind, shall strive by teaching and education to promote respect for these rights and freedoms and by progressive measures, national and international, to secure their universal and effective recognition and observance, both among the peoples of Member States themselves and among the <u>peoples of territories under their jurisdiction</u>".

People under their jurisdiction, this declaration places indigenous people that have been colonized by invaders under the rule of foreigners and their systems. That is slavery.

In the coming years, it would become very clear that the UN declaration was insufficient and lacking in protections for indigenous peoples around the world. So, indigenous and other concerned people would release a barrage of proposals, declaration, covenants, and recommendations aimed toward equality for indigenous peoples around the world. If the original Declaration had been comprehensive, there would be no need for instruments like...

1. The UN Indigenous and Tribal Populations Convention and Recommendation 104 ... 1957

2. The UN Covenant on Economic Social and Cultural Rights 1966

3. The UN Indigenous and Tribal Peoples Convention, 1989 (No. 169) *concerning Indigenous and Tribal Peoples in Independent Countries (Entry into force: 05 Sep 1991) Adoption: Geneva, 76th ILC session (27 Jun 1989) - Status: Up-to-date instrument (Technical Convention). Convention may be denounced: 05 Sep 2021 - 05 Sep 2022*

4. The Mund Bareefan Clan -Indigenous Native American Association of Nations Constitution... State Acknowledgement entered into effect in the State of Georgia, March 3rd, 2003; Federal Acknowledgement entered into effect in the United States February 11th, 2004.

5. The UN Declaration of the Rights of Indigenous Peoples 13 September 2007

These instruments were brought forth after the Universal Declaration of Human Rights. Some of these proposals have been signed and ratified by the United Nations General Assembly, some have not.

However, these type instruments along with international court cases and other existing agreements that we have made that speak to the issues at hand, are the tools that indigenous people should use to enter negotiations with others. Here is a rhetorical question. If the Declaration was written for the rights of all humans, then why were the subsequent instruments needed? Why not just amend it? That's two questions.

C107 - Indigenous and Tribal Populations Convention, 1957 (No. 107)

Convention concerning the Protection and Integration of Indigenous and Other Tribal and Semi-Tribal Populations in Independent Countries (Entry into force: 02 Jun 1959) Adoption: Geneva, 40th ILC session (26 Jun 1957) - Status: Outdated instrument (Technical Convention). Convention may be denounced: 02 Jun 2019 - 02 Jun 2020

The General Conference of the International Labor Organization,

Having been convened at Geneva by the Governing Body of the International Labour Office, and having met in its Fortieth Session on 5 June 1957, and

Having decided upon the adoption of certain proposals with regard to the protection and integration of indigenous and other tribal and semi-tribal populations in independent countries, which is the sixth item on the agenda of the session, and

Having determined that these proposals shall take the form of an international Convention, and

Considering that the Declaration of Philadelphia affirms that all human beings have the right to pursue both their material well-being and their spiritual development in conditions of freedom and dignity, of economic security and equal opportunity, and

Considering that there exist in various independent countries indigenous and other tribal and semi-tribal populations which are not yet integrated into the national community and whose social, economic or cultural situation hinders them from benefiting fully from the rights and advantages enjoyed by other elements of the population, and

Considering it desirable both for humanitarian reasons and in the interest of the countries concerned to promote continued action to improve the living and working conditions of these populations by simultaneous action in respect of all the factors which have hitherto prevented them from sharing fully in the progress of the national community of which they form part, and

<u>Considering that the adoption of general international standards on the subject will facilitate action to assure the protection of the populations concerned, their progressive integration into their respective national communities, and the improvement of their living and working conditions,</u> and

Noting that these standards have been framed with the co-operation of the United Nations, the Food and Agriculture Organization of the United Nations, the United Nations Educational, Scientific and Cultural Organization and the World Health Organization, at appropriate levels and in their respective fields, and that it is proposed to seek their continuing co-operation in promoting and securing the application of these standards, adopts this twenty-sixth day of June of the year one thousand nine hundred and fifty-seven the following Convention, which may be cited as the Indigenous and Tribal Populations Convention, 1957:

PART I. GENERAL POLICY

Article 1

1. This Convention applies to--

(a) members of tribal or <u>semi-tribal</u> populations in independent countries whose social and economic conditions are at a less advanced stage than the stage reached by the other sections of the national community, and whose status is regulated wholly or partially by their own customs or traditions or by special laws or regulations;

(b) members of tribal or semi-tribal populations in independent countries which are regarded as indigenous on account of their descent from the populations which inhabited the country, or a geographical region to which the country belongs, at the time of conquest or colonization and which, irrespective of their legal status, live more in conformity with the social, economic and cultural institutions of that time than with the institutions of the nation to which they belong.

2. For the purposes of this Convention, the term *semi-tribal* includes groups and persons who, although they are in the process of losing their tribal characteristics, are not yet integrated into the national community.

3. The indigenous and other tribal or semi-tribal populations mentioned in paragraphs 1 and 2 of this Article are referred to hereinafter as "the populations concerned".

Let's look at article 1 point 2 of Indigenous and Tribal Populations Convention, (No. 107) 1957

"The term semi-tribal: Article 1 point 2:   For the purposes of this Convention, the term includes groups and persons who, although they are in the process of losing their tribal characteristics, are not yet integrated into the national community."

If you meet someone and they tell you that they have a grandmother, grandfather, an uncle, aunt, mother, father, who informed them that they had some "Indian" blood in them, (meaning Indigenous American Blood) then semi-tribal means them.

If your ancestors are/were indigenous and call you yourself Latino American, Black American, African American, or anything like that, congratulations you are no longer semi-tribal. You have successfully integrated into the US national community. It may just be, that that person is just exercising their right to personal self-determination, or maybe they're not.   Hmmm!!!

Indigenous Peoples may not have considered, yet in this day in time, we should consider our position in the world as "Acknowledged" and or "Recognized" autonomous peoples by the independent governments that occupy our ancestral lands or lands we lawfully occupy and by other governments around the world.

Or, you may still be under the misconception that, The Universal Declaration of Human Rights, at the time of the writing, was written with "Indigenous Peoples," "African Americans", and other "Peoples of Color" in mind. The Universal Declaration did not "see" in the legal sense, our governments, clans, tribes, alliances, or associations. We were not seen as autonomous, and parties to said Declaration. Those governments only saw/see us as under their jurisdictions.

House Thunderbird, that is our family, and many other families in New York and Pennsylvania began our quest as autonomous people in the mid-70s. We were members of a religious society called The Ansar Allah Community. We owned land, property, farms, and made other businesses. We built entire communities. We bound together and set a spark that reflected from coast to coast in the United States. Then things changed.

Our Mund Bareefan family continued, not in a religious institution but by legal action toward recognition through our birthright as the indigenous family we are.

Most of us old heads first got into the legal quest for recognition of autonomy in the 1970's, we just didn't know what it was. Twenty plus years later, we found ourselves reading tools like "Breaking the Code". I read and for a short period of time, a very short time, I used the "Breaking the Code" publications. This was the "Sovereignty Movement".

Think about it, you walk into a courtroom and present your documentation to the Judge, documentation which states that the courtroom that you just have entered, and the sitting Judge is without jurisdiction over you. First, the judge needs to determine if you are a foreigner. Well, guess what? Legally speaking you are not a foreigner, but you already knew that. You are a US American citizen.

Anyway... next, the case may be about international commerce, or negotiable paper, or taxes; and your brief is loaded with US CODE, FRCP, UCC, rules of evidence or some other United States protocols which cannot relate to you nor to the court in relation to you, other than as a US citizen.

Why? Remember that you presented documents to the court that outlines that you are foreign to their jurisdiction. You told them you are your own jurisdiction; or under the jurisdiction of some other entity. As a foreigner, you, the real live flesh and blood human which I am, we all are, have no standing to bring this type case before their court. As the American the court sees you, you can be detained or incarcerated and sentenced to do time.

First, as an indigenous person, you should not have reason to be in their court. That's another lesson. If you take yourself there and your brief is loaded with the above authorities as your principle support, do you realize that you are using their shields or someone else's as your protection? Things that make you go, Hmmm!!!

This practice is used with the "Sovereignty Movement". These tactics were developed by factions of the "Patriot Movement". I never use this term (sovereignty) anymore. This is not for us. It is not the type of law for us. It is too combative, and it is an adversary to "Reflective Humanism". These tactics are about the individual, not about "We".

www.ingramcontent.com/pod-product-compliance
Lightning Source LLC
Chambersburg PA
CBHW041527090426
42736CB00035B/41